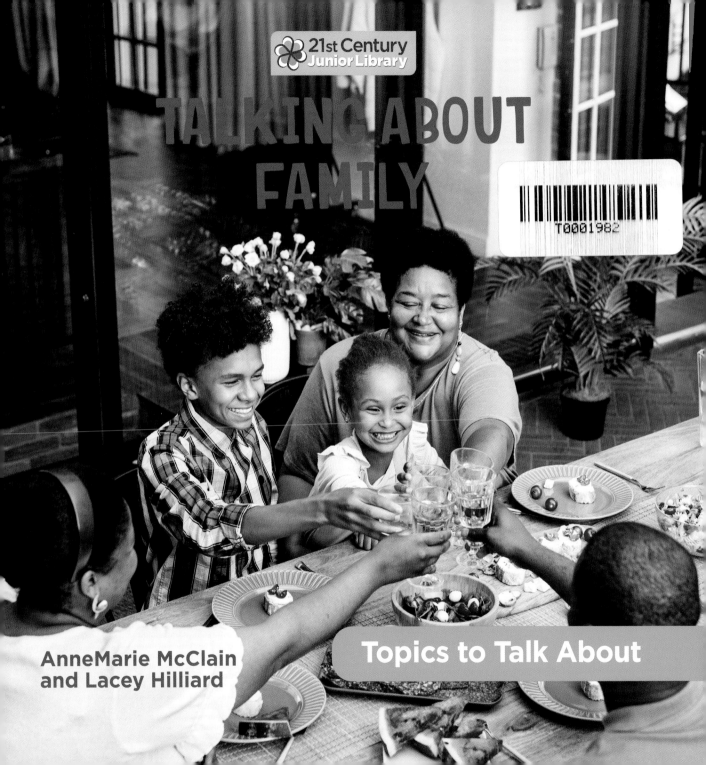

21st Century Junior Library

TALKING ABOUT FAMILY

AnneMarie McClain
and Lacey Hilliard

Topics to Talk About

Published in the United States of America by Cherry Lake Publishing Group
Ann Arbor, Michigan
www.cherrylakepublishing.com

Reading Adviser: Beth Walker Gambro, MS, Ed., Reading Consultant, Yorkville, IL
Book Designer: Jen Wahi

Photo Credits: Cover: © SeventyFour/Shutterstock; page 5: © True Touch Lifestyle/Shutterstock; page 6: © Da Antipina/ Shutterstock; page 7: © fizkes/Shutterstock; page 8: © fizkes/Shutterstock; page 9: © Day Of Victory Studio/Shutterstock; page 9 (bottom left): © Rido/Shutterstock; page 9 (bottom right): fizkes/Shutterstock; page 10: © Monkey Business Images/ Shutterstock; page 11: © Roman Chazov/Shutterstock; page 12–13: © Evgeny Atamanenko/Shutterstock; page 14 (left): © Natasha_Chetkova/Shutterstock; page 14 (right): © stockpexel/Shutterstock; page 15: © Odua Images/Shutterstock; page 16: © Narint Asawaphisith/Shutterstock; page 18 (left): © Auttapol Tatiyarat/Shutterstock; page 18 (right): © Denis Kuvaev/ Shutterstock; page 19: © FedorAnisimov/Shutterstock; page 20–21: © Monkey Business Images/Shutterstock

Library of Congress Cataloging-in-Publication Data

Names: Hilliard, Lacey, author. | McClain, AnneMarie, author.
Title: Talking about family / written by: Lacey Hilliard and AnneMarie McClain.
Description: Ann Arbor, Michigan : Cherry Lake Publishing, [2023] | Series: Topics to talk about | Audience: Grades 2-3 | Summary: "How do we talk about the different ways that families can look? This book breaks down the topic of family for young readers. Filled with engaging photos and captions, this series opens up opportunities for deeper thought and informed conversation. Guided exploration of topics in 21st Century Junior Library's signature style help readers to Look, Think, Ask Questions, Make Guesses, and Create as they go!"– Provided by publisher.
Identifiers: LCCN 2022039672 | ISBN 9781668919316 (hardcover) | ISBN 9781668920336 (paperback) | ISBN 9781668921661 (ebook) | ISBN 9781668922996 (pdf)
Subjects: LCSH: Families–Psychological aspects–Juvenile literature. | Interpersonal relations–Psychological aspects–Juvenile literature. | Communication in families–Juvenile literature.
Classification: LCC HQ519 .H55 2023 | DDC 306.85–dc23/eng/20220818
LC record available at https://lccn.loc.gov/2022039672

Cherry Lake Publishing would like to acknowledge the work of the Partnership for 21st Century Learning, a network of Battelle for Kids. Please visit *http://www.battelleforkids.org/networks/p21* for more information.

Printed in the United States of America
Corporate Graphics

CHERRY LAKE PRESS

CONTENTS

TALKING ABOUT FAMILY

A family can be any number of people. Sometimes there is one grown-up in a family. Sometimes two or more. Sometimes families have no children. Sometimes they have one, two, or more.

Grown-ups can be parents, grandparents, aunts, uncles, siblings, cousins, or other caring adults. Families can also include pets. There is also what some people call a "chosen family." A chosen family

Each family can look different. There is no ONE way a family needs to be!

has people chosen to love and be close to like family.

Sometimes people in families look the same. Sometimes they don't. Some families are large. Some are small. Some families all live in one home. Some live spread out in more than one home. Some families combine with other families to create a bigger family.

Some families have children, or more than one child. Some families don't. All kinds of families are good.

Look!

Look at all of these loving families! They are doing so much together. What do you notice about these families? What seems the same? What seems different?

Kids can be part of families. Some kids are born into their families. Foster families take care of kids who are waiting for a family they can stay with forever. Some kids are adopted into their families. Kids who are adopted needed a family and then found one. All kids deserve to be loved in their families.

Divorce can be a part of families, too. Divorce is when grown-ups decide to stop being married to each other. If a family has a divorce, it can feel hard. It's never the kid's fault.

Families can have different amounts of money and things. Some families have a lot of money, and some families have less. Some families buy new things. Some buy or get things that have been used before. Some families live in big houses. Some families live in smaller houses, apartments, mobile homes, shelters, or other places. Some families are looking for a place to call home.

Families can be different.
Every family is unique.

9

Families live in all different ways. All families should be treated equally. It shouldn't matter how much money or how many things they have. It shouldn't matter how new their clothes and things are or where they live.

There are many kinds of families, and they can all be equally full of love.

Some people have multiple generations in their family. They may have parents and grandparents. They may even have great-grandparents!

Some people have more than one race in their family. A study done in 2015 found that 11 million people have a spouse of a different race or ethnicity.

KIDS AND FAMILY

Families are important to kids, no matter what they look like.

No families do everything exactly the same. People are different, and that's great! There are many ways to show love in a family. An important way is to do the best they can to keep their kids safe and to give them what they need. This can look different in each family.

Make a Guess!

What do you think your family will look like when you are a grown-up? What would make your family feel safe and loved?

Right now, you are a kid in a family. Your family will change over your life.

One day, you will be a grown-up. You might want a family for yourself. If you would like, you can find someone you love to be part of your family. You can also choose to have a child or a pet. Then you would be a parent to a child or the care person for an animal. You can have a chosen family any time, too!

There are families of all different cultures and religions!

About 135,000 children are adopted in the U.S. every year.

WHAT'S MOST IMPORTANT TO REMEMBER?

Families can look different and be different.
There are many ways that families are the same, too.
Families can change, and families can stay the same.
Part of the changing can happen as you grow up.

Think!

What is your family like?
What do you like to do together?

REFLECTING ABOUT FAMILY

Think about a friend that you have. Who is in their family? What do they like to do as a family? What are some of the ways that your families are the same? What are some ways that your families are different?

What is something you would like the grown-ups at your school to do to help kids with all kinds of families feel included?

What is something you could do in your community to help kids with different kinds of families feel included?

Create!

Draw something exciting you want to do with your family. What would you do? Where would you be? This can be something that your family has done before or something that you might want to do. It's okay if you cannot actually do it with your family. It can be pretend!

Ask Questions!

Family can mean different things to different people. Find a teacher or family member and ask them what family means to them. Then talk about what family means to you.

What kind of family do you think you want to have when you are older? Do you think you want to have a pet?

GLOSSARY

adopted (uh-DAHP-tuhd) legally becoming part of a family

chosen family (CHOH-zuhn FAHM-lee) people who are not related by blood but form a family group

divorce (duh-VORSS) act of legally ending a marriage

foster families (FAW-stuhr FAHM-leez) families who care for children when their parents are unable to care for them

LEARN MORE

Book: *A Family Is a Family Is a Family* by Sara O'Leary (2016)
https://www.redleafpress.org/A-Family-Is-a-Family-Is-a-Family-P1745.aspx

Video: AMAZE.org "Different Kinds of Families" (2019, ~3 mins)
https://www.youtube.com/watch?v=hpCyiyNqzlE

Video (with a grown-up): ABC ME "What It's Like Having Same-Sex Parents" (2018, ~7 min) https://www.youtube.com/watch?v=4KGOobnZjvE

INDEX

ABOUT THE AUTHORS

AnneMarie K. McClain is an educator, researcher, and parent. Her work is about how kids and families can feel good about who they are. She especially loves finding ways to help kids and families feel seen in TV and books.

Lacey J. Hilliard is a college professor, researcher, and parent. Her work is in understanding how grown-ups talk to children about the world around them. She particularly likes hearing what kids have to say about things.